Copyright © 2024 by Pippa Bird

All rights reserved. No part of this book may be reproduced or transmitted in any form or by any means, electronic or mechanical, including photocopying, recording, or by any information storage and retrieval system, without permission in writing from the publisher.

ISBN: 9781763753204

First Edition

I0149366

Unwind with
Calm Kangaroo

Written & Illustrated by Pippa Bird

Hi, my name is Kirri, and I am the Calm Kangaroo.
I like to practise being calm and mindful. It is my favourite
thing to do.

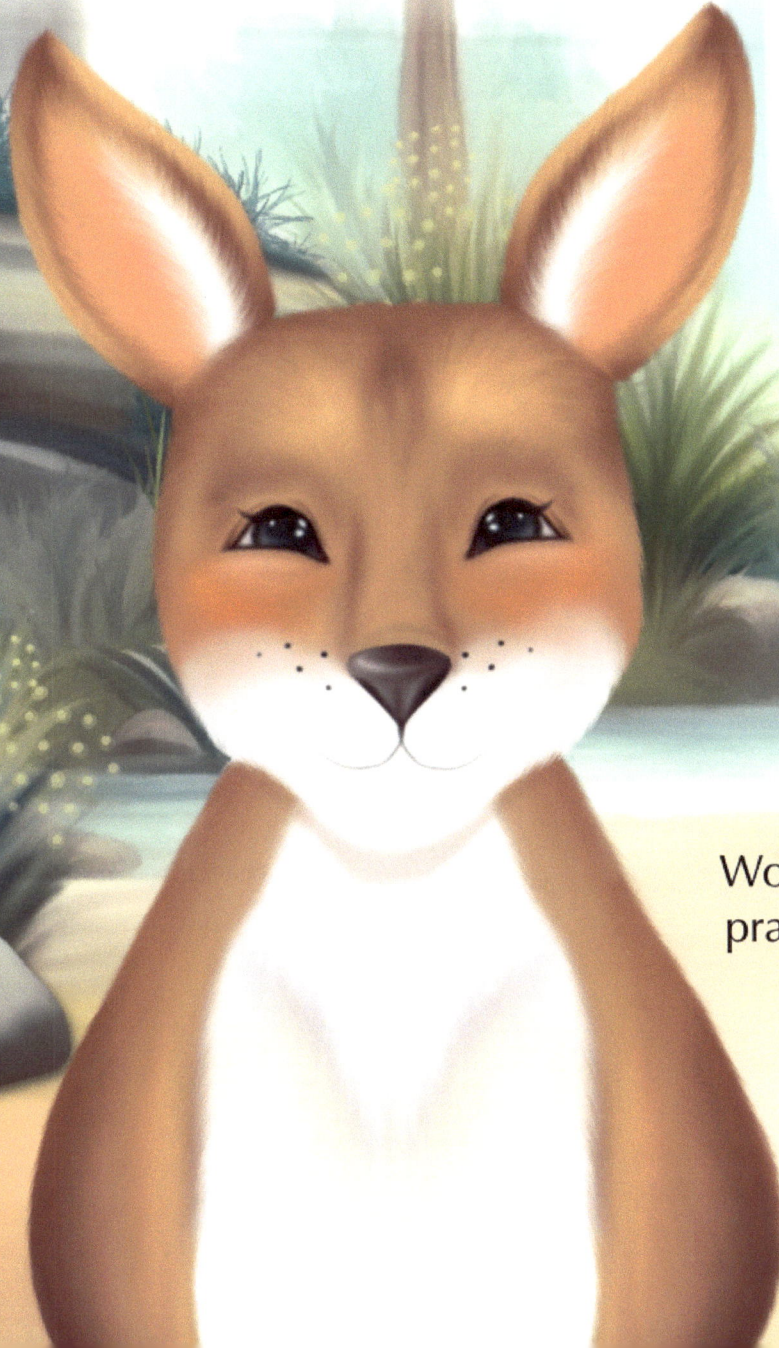

Would you like to
practise with me?

First, let's place both of our feet firmly on the ground. Like this.

Next, we close our eyes like this.

Next, we need to focus on our breathing. In and out.
In and out. Slowly and calmly.

Now we're ready to stretch and unwind.

Balance and peace, we find within.
Lotus roo, where we begin.

In a quiet space, where worries unwind.
We stretch and breathe, to calm our mind.

With each deep breath, we feel the flow.
Inhale peace, let tension go.

Balancing roo, we stand and sway.
Chest open wide, we greet the day.

Warrior roo, we feel the ground.
In this moment, we are safe and sound.

Don't forget to keep breathing slowly and calmly.
In and out. In and out.

With every pose, our worries fade.
In this practice, calm is made.

Crouching roo, we rest and breathe.
In the stillness, our mind at ease.

Cobra roo breathing deep, we find our way.
To a peaceful heart, where we can stay.

Resting roo, our stretch is done.
Peaceful mind, calm has begun.

Was that fun?
Are you
feeling calm?

I love stretching and breathing to help me practise being calm. I can practise anywhere. And so can you!

I can practise in the Red Centre,
Right next to Uluru.

I can practise on a walk,
With a friend or two.

I can practise in a field of yellow,
Breathe in, let go, unwind.

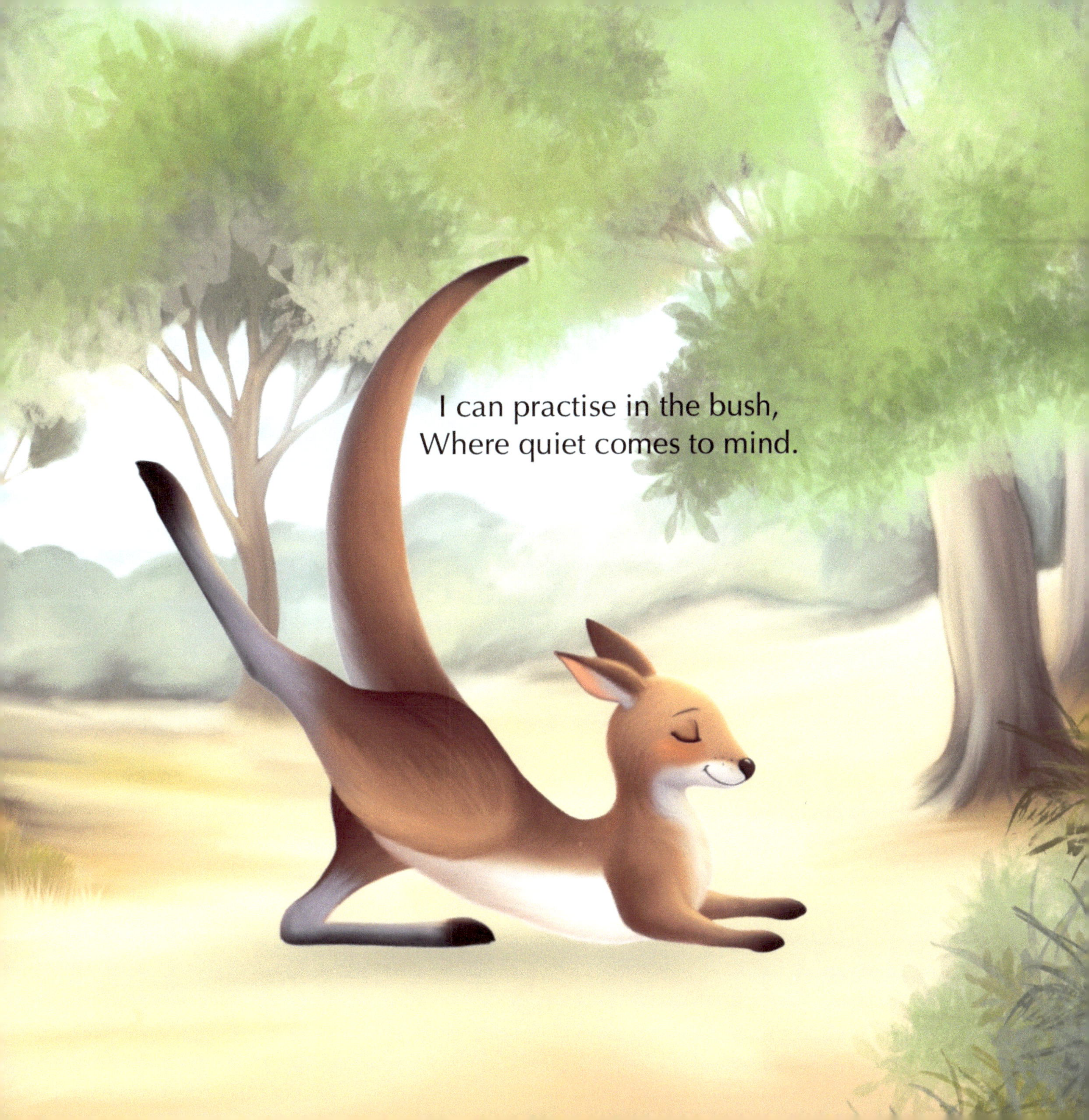

I can practise in the bush,
Where quiet comes to mind.

I can practise anywhere,
Here, there, near and far.

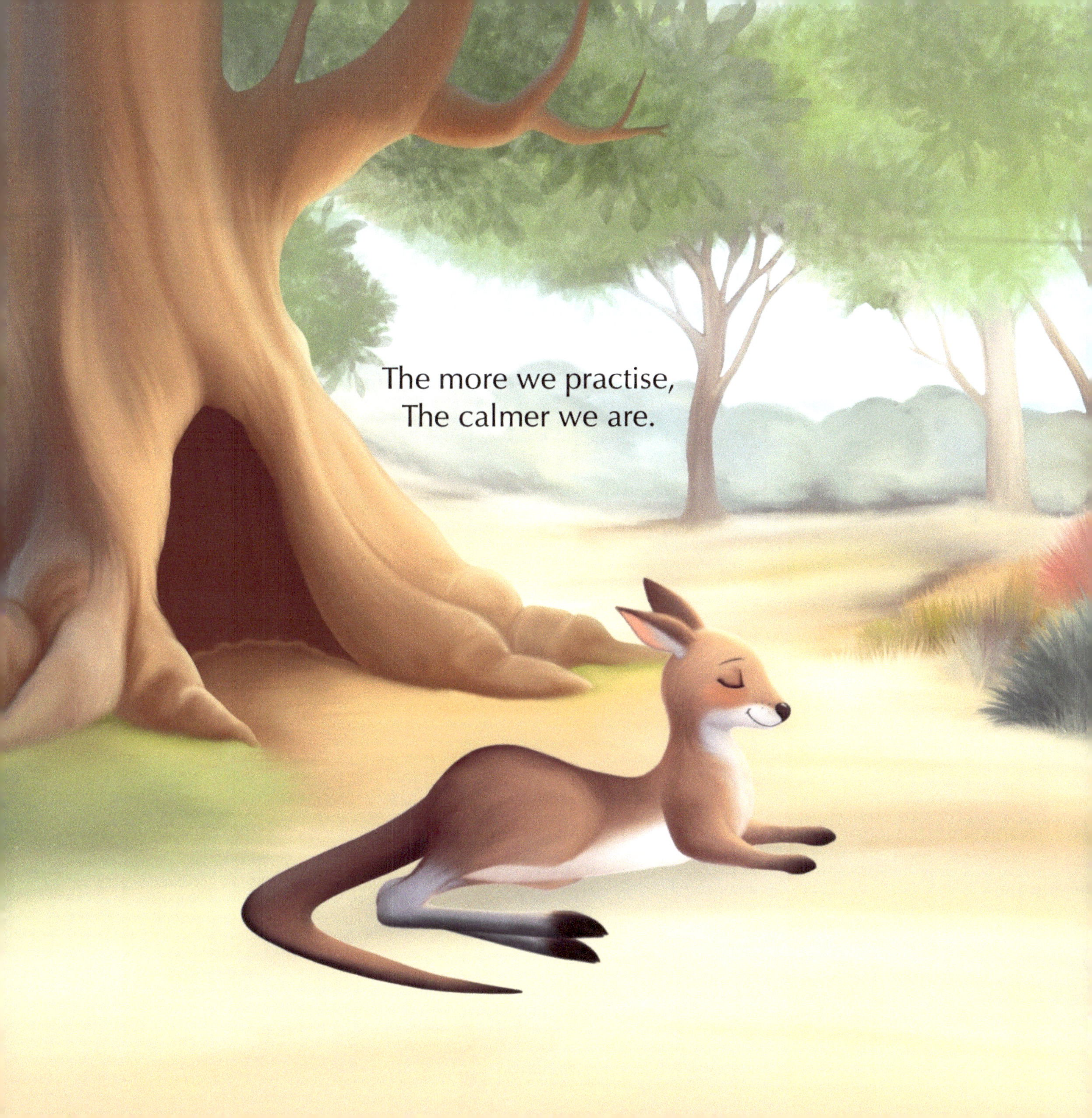

The more we practise,
The calmer we are.

Now that you know how to be calm, you can practise every day. Next time we'll take a walk together, I'll be happy to show you the way.

Lotus Roo

Bridge Roo

Boat Roo

Here is my guide to help
you practise your poses.
Don't forget to breathe.
In and out. In and out.

Warrior Roo

Flag Roo

Balancing Roo

Cobra Roo

Crouching Roo

Resting Roo

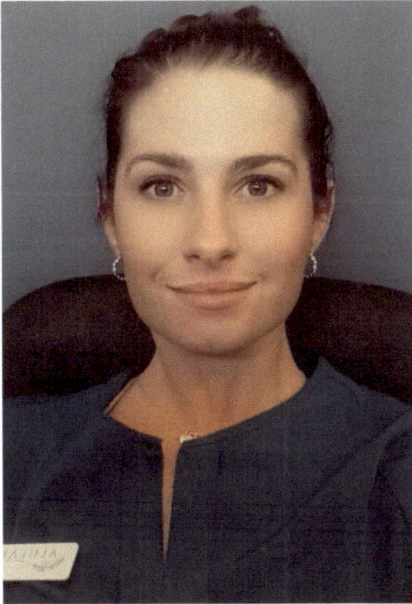

Calm Kangaroo

About the Author

Pippa Bird is a Mental Health Therapist in Private Practice in regional NSW. Pippa holds a Bachelor in Psychology, a Diploma in Counselling, and is currently undertaking a Postgraduate Degree in the field.

Pippa also holds a Diploma in Graphic Design, with a primary focus on illustration.

CALM KANGAROO is a backronym title for a children's mental well-being program. An initiative designed to educate children about mental health and foster a learning journey of emotional intelligence, resilience and cultivate an open mind through the power of reading well-being books, leading to the most important discussions and ideas.

The CALM KANGAROO program focuses on **C**urating, **A**dvocating and **L**eading **M**indfulness and its mission to **K**indle **A**wareness, **N**urture **G**rowth, **A**mplify **R**esilience, and **O**rchestrate **O**pen-minds.

ALULA BLU
COUNSELLING SERVICES

Calm Kangaroo is an Alula Blu Initiative

www.ingramcontent.com/pod-product-compliance
Lightning Source LLC
LaVergne TN
LVHW072112070426
835509LV00003B/127

9 781763 753204